Terracom Poet Series

I0162839

Child's Play

William Driscoll

Terracom Books

Child's Play
Terracom Books Poetry Series/March 2014
First Edition

Published by Terracom Books
A Division of Terracom Media

ISBN–13: 978–0–615–96858–2

Terracom Media

mediaterracom@gmail.com
angel

CONTENTS

The Child

The Poet of Sen Sel-Amar

Preface

At the age of six, I was reciting Longfellow's "The Skeleton in Armor," from memory. Shortly would follow Wordsworth, then Tennyson, then Byron. My maternal grandfather, an Olympic gymnast, a sheriff, a self–educated lawyer, an elected judge and a commemorated race car mechanic for Louis Chevrolet in the early days of the Indianapolis 500, was also a lover (of poetry) and the books he gave me, yellowing tomes with his own favorite lines lightly underlined, were to stir in me a love of antique verse and sow the seeds of my juvenilia.

I dreamt of a world more than a hundred of years gone (if it ever existed). My thoughts were the thoughts of that age: the heroic, the transitory and the grave. In 1975, after writing a slew of overly sentimental love poems to a round redheaded girl at school, I wrote a shaky Shakespearean sonnet stating:

> *The words I wrote in love are not the same*
> *I read them now no fire in heart is stirred*

And destroyed these early efforts in entirety.

For the next eight years, I would turn my youthful energies to the task of revitalizing, resuscitating and modernizing antique forms sans dripping sentimentality, to reinstate rhythm and rhyme to their proper place. A task doomed to failure? Perhaps. But what could be more romantic? Poems came to me in chaotic bursts and true to the romantic tradition, I recorded them faithfully, suffering little revision as the years went by. But sadly, and inevitably, I too soon grew up and left such romance (for the most part) in memory.

In 1983, as I had invariably played out the ballad, the sonnet and the lay, as well as many external and internal rhymes possible in the English language (and some that weren't possible), I came to a precipice of choice. No longer satisfied to write in this fashion, I was faced with a terrible decision, whether to conform to a modern school of poetry or to strike out and seek alternate forms. Despite this rift, I would never forget the zest, zeal and passion of that early poetry. If, as has been written, wisdom is the compensation for lost youth then when I gain some, perhaps I will feel less melancholy for the loss.

I make no excuse for my use of archaisms in these poems or antique concepts. Form must follow content and content form, as a young romantic must be true to their ideals.

To all those lost romantics struggling to find meaning in our modern age, to all those truly young or still young enough at heart to appreciate them, I dedicate my youthful verses.

W.D.

St. Petersburg, Florida
June, 1989

The Child

Time's Test

The Night – Cold, Black, Worried

The Boy – Warm, Dark, Hurried

The Girl – Cool, Light, Away

The Love – Old, Fight, Scurried

The Test – Hot, Hard, Play

The list goes on and ends in this way:

A phone rings

a light is remembered

a song sings

it's again cool September

a hurried hand

lifts the U

and darkly replaces

the chance was too few

black slowly passes

in its worried way

and the two side's

long fight

enters the play

the dark fights the light

for control of the sky

each morn

the struggles renew

only in black

may the two share the sky

and then the hard question

sounded is "Why?"

the dark answers

'the chance was too few'

the cold lingers on

the warm wishing its end

light to befriend

the hot cries them down

the scurried hard play

is away on the ground

Let us cease the Talk of Autumn

Let us cease the talk of autumn
till the snow lay on the ground
the leaves must fall it's told us
and December must come 'round
but I'm a disbeliever
my mind is tightly closed
all I see are trees a' flowering
spreading seedlings in their rows

This is not your first spring
your last with autumn died
you can't forget the shining sun
since last you did espy
but now spring is renewing
and a blinking meets your eye
at dusk my fire's kindled
reach out – Yes! – catch this fly

No sun, my light, dim–bright
will melt winter's ice
from your hesitant heart
and so impart
that spring's returned
lush and verdant green

renewing winds rustling

the eaves serene

But the months will pass

time will not cease

let love bring life

till love release

for the dew will dry

in summer's heat

and leaves will fall brown

at our feet

But of autumn today

I will not speak

till winter's sleep

our love does meet

I Search through a Myriad of Phantoms

I search through a myriad of phantoms
for a glass shard in the Sahara sands
I can't feel the real from illusions
with the calluses tough on my hands

The dark and the light in the dark or the light
look the same
it seems the stars, dim–bright
look the same

And in the world the women look the same
don't ask me why, I can't explain

A glimpse of light, a light foot fall
I've seen them countless
I've heard them all
an heir of Tantalus, I've tried to reach
a retreating wave across a beach

And in the world the women look the same
don't ask me why, I can't explain

I search through a legacy of shadow
for a light that is lost in the land
but I'm greeted by storms in the dessert
with the force that such meetings demand

The known and forgotten in the moment of learning

look the same

the images I see of sorrow and yearning

look the same

And in the world the lovers look the same

don't ask me why, I can't explain...

Celestial Beings feel not the Things

Celestial beings feel not the things
mortals, we must feel
and see not the sights that cast dim doubt
and swirl our mortal minds about

God and goddess, intrigue, entwined
read lightly the tapestry the years unwind
know that pain is ephemeral swift forgot
care not that human flesh must rot

Love makes monarchs and reigns of bliss
but kingdoms crumble when love's remiss
the gods know not the fall of men
but love and love and love again

Pedestal and bust will turn to dust
but beings eternal have endless lust

Dream god-like, love, for dreams can be
the key to the cell that sets us free
from fear of failure or understandings lost
or paying the unending human cost

At the table of our joy must sorrow be seated
agony accepted, frustration greeted?

must we allow the tearing of our soft love's soul

by carrion forces we can't control?

Like deity and deity, we must mend with sight

and set these human–mistakes to right

then will we know the amour of gods

and beat time's weary weighted odds

I Wonder Sometimes

I wonder sometimes if it will be lasting
like the lingering bite of fine food to the fasting
a morsel of memory with times added taste
that no reality of spoilage can mold or abase

Those nights mean nothing when we can't feel the heat
and we send ourselves running to distant retreats
riddled with a petty perpetuating force
looking for longing amid the remorse

A kiss on the corners, two lips parted slightly
we're searching for loving and searching quite rightly
but the meaning and order cause us to waiver
forgetting the moments we needed to savor

The motions of desire burn to fine ash
leaving us syllables tattered and brash
the insane and the sane struggle within us
as we ponder the presence of the innocent and sinless

We mend each other's moments but the fabric is brittle
weakening with straining little by little
why must we look for our long lost humanity?
augmenting the accusing of our hopeless insanity

The rational and irrational, both councils we take
and rational and irrational mistakes we both make
we wait out our winters racing at random
leaving our loving alone and abandoned

We fight and surrender with the same solemn sigh
missing the meaning as we question the sky
some day we'll know better why we must run
but then our delightful young dash will be done

To List the Things I Admire

To list the things I admire in my lover
would be a task indeed
for the she I perceive is beyond my craft
and so it would require infinite drafts
for it to seem what I'd wish it to be

She touches me at times with her deeps at the depth
of the subtle sign language we've formed
we carry on discussions beneath the entangled
words that seem flat and forlorn

I know her
it's strange to realize
but I recognize what's behind her gaze
and share the increasing weight of her days
I like her
it's strange to say

She watches and wonders at the sights of her sight
and dwells on the questions of life
we define the differences as we share the experiences
and debate the great findings we find

Not that we're not in love
I assure you

there's no other but my lover

for me

And when we're at peace

my lover knows too

that what we've got is a blessing

really

I'm sure she'll enjoy this awkward expression

for she'll know that it comes from my inward
affection

but when talking, quite frankly

about the lines that you see

I'm afraid that my lover and I won't agree

The Higher you Build

The higher you build
your tower of truth
the farther into falsehood
it falls
the longer you delay
the longing of right
the thicker you mortar
the wall
the more you lose touch
with the tides of your sea
the faster the fools
flock around
they slowly step blindly
in piles of debris
where there's no solid ground
to be found
you can run with some passion
collaged with fine fashion
you can look for a life
you can win
but in your mind there's a maze
that none can appraise

though you don't like to blunder

within

look! the tall trees are swaying

the small deaths decaying

the children are singing

of dearth

the mute men are saying

to speak is depressing

and totally lacking

in worth

you must come taste the fruit

of the blind, deaf and mute

you'll be satiate on truth

in this lie

then the sand-crust will close

your eyes, mouth and nose

and with a longing for living

you'll die

The Cove

The hidden path is steep and slick
but sure are the feet that carry us down
by bending branch and trap and trick
our sorrow in the sea to drown

Dark moods, dark clothes, a questing glance
a world that looks at life askance
we seek the sea, serenity
we dance our dark and dire degree

Fork by fork a feat complete
we near the central spot
the moonlight whispers, 'be discreet'
the sand says 'forget not!'

Dark eyes, dark news, the altered moods
a world that feasts on fetid foods
we seek the change, rearrange
we eagerly enter our eerie exchange

Over the rocks of our reason
we balance and shift
anticipating the sacred sand
where the moon–maiden waits
the wind worrying her shrift

and the sea soundly sleeps

in her hand

Dark night, dark time, a sigh sublime

a world that's forgotten a simpler time

we seek the trip, re–equip

we solemnly sail our fantasy ship

To an altar that sits in a sea bordered cove

with woods to the left rear and right

there two ghosts are seated in silence to prove

that the end of our geas is in sight

Slow stride, quick pace, no sighs of disgrace

from a world that loves the common place

we come through smoke

to where the ancients spoke

and the laws of living are ours to revoke

The ghosts of the soldier, curtal–maid–and–thief

sit there at the table of raw nature's feast

they care little that their time is short

or that the night must still transport

them back to the world from whence they came

where they must remember an unrecalled name . . .

Dark thens, dark nows, the proud head bows

a world that's forgotten its whys and hows

we seek recourse for remorse

we ride a wild yet fettered horse

The Child

As I walk again the flat–stone street
the mist permeates my skin
leading me to the round rinse–rooms
where the mist is squeezed into mold
and the story of the crack in the wall
is told

As I sit withdrawn on a singe–soaked floor
I mutter, 'open a window, throw open a door'
my need is a sore I need to efface
for I'm trapped in a dark and dusky place

As I stumble on my beat–battered feet
the night grows dense in my brain
I seem like a man shunning a hand
but willing to walk with a cane

As I gaze at the portrait of the child, I plead
for an answer to a question
an insight, I need
the child smiles and replies
'you subsist on lies –
there's no answers worth wanting'
the child replies

'But tell me, old youth

as I stand here myself

why do I stand on my knees?'

the child smiles and replies

'too wide is your pride

too seldom you've tried to appease'

So I keep it inside as I laugh and I cry

to see the child so wild is me!

but he smiles and replies

'too often you hide'

as I left him he told me I'd see

The Poet of Sen Sel–Amar

Halwin's Search

Through woods both dense and dark by day
the young lord journeyed on his way
from sea to sea he looked upon
the lands beyond fair Galadon

When day was done and night was full
awoke he slew marauding wolves
then washed his arms in a winding brook
'midst outlands that the lords forsook

This for what he sought to find
those varied wonders dreamed behind
those walls that close that plateau high
with pools that still reflect the sky

Due north he stalked the wild elk
with stealth he skinned the black wolf's pelt
he journeyed long amidst the trees
and swam in wild wanton seas

When day was full he came upon
men that knew not Galadon
in naked fear they hid from him
who had not hate nor fright nor sin

With voice that rang both bright and clear
he called to them to calm their fear
"Come to me O! scion of man
come join my search to understand!"

That kingly knight thou maverick lord
went on to tame the wild horde
that roamed the endless forests free
from Suncrest's spires to crystal sea

The hunter wild then built new walls
and dreamed new dreams in wooden halls
they flocked to him and hailed him king
in times when forests filled in spring

In his long day the deeds he's done
in many a stately song is sung
of this brave lord that reigned beyond
the land that men called Galadon

The Poet of Sen Sel–Amar

All are architects of Fate,
Working in these walls of Time;
Some with massive deeds and great,
Some with ornaments of rhyme.
~Longfellow

'I am the poet of Sen Sel–Amar

hearken me people from near and afar

come to me children of Sen Sel–Amar

and hear what I would say

'I am known as the poet of Sen Sel–Amar

but I come from the kingdom Penelopus–Tar

where poets are persecuted thrown to the hounds

and the woeful's doleful injustice abounds

'Oh my dark kingdom in the dark hills of doubt

where lyric and limerick are strictly cut out

of all would be poets dear Sen Sel–Amar

now hear of the land of my youth

'I was an urchin of ten, a rhyme did I make

and for my small laugh a finger they did take

from my knuckle, to teach me of Penelopus–Tar

the land in the dark hills where no poets are

'You see poets were banned by the queen in a rage

when succeeding in finding her like on a page

of poetry infamous in Penelopus–Tar
a satire posted by Regius Lazar

'Regius was buried in the woods they say
and the lords outlawed poetry that very same day
there I was a lad and rhymes were my joy
so quickly I became a finger–less boy

'As I grew older I kept my mouth shut
for I knew not which digit next would be cut
but I rhymed in my head as I lay in my bed
and the fire in my chest grew robust and red

'When into my manhood they trusted me not
(for my love of the limerick was not forgot)
to damn the source of my creative springs
they put out my eyes with two red hot rings

'Oh my life then was lonely dear Sen Sel–Amar
in the land in the dark hills where no poets are

'I begged for my livelihood and bided my time
while still in my head I continued to rhyme
for my spirit wasn't broken as days went their way
'twas my wit that preserved me despite the decay

'One day, I convinced a young lad to write down my lines
and out of my head I dredged up my rhymes

I bid him then post them in the kingdom's confines
the kingdom of Penelopus-Tar

'Then when I was hunted by guards in the night
far from the dark hills I stumbled in flight
I was led by my lad to the shores of this sea
Sen Sel-Amar where poets are free!

'On that first day I stood here my words turned to song
and you came and you gathered and listened quite long
to all the joy lain lost in my pain
soon Sen Sel-Amar you joined my refrain

'You fed me, embraced me and soothed the scar
of my journey from boyhood in Penelopus-Tar
you called me the poet of Sen Sel-Amar
and long have I lingered among you

'Now as I stand on these shores at the end of my days
dwelling on the passing of countless by-ways
and the poor queen's commands for spite of my verse
that was meant as a kinder reminder of mirth

'Come, grieve with me people from near and afar
for the happiness silenced in Penelopus-Tar...'

Saying this the poet faced straight out to sea
as if on the white waves he could be free

then slumping to sitting with one short breath
the poet set sail for the kingdom of death

There still he cites lines to all who will hear
some laugh at his rhymes and pass in good cheer
but for some he saves the tale of Penelopus–Tar
the land in the dark hills where no poets are

Song of Renfrew

A young lad rode
on the highway one day
foot taut in the stirrup
stroking his bay
he rode to the city
to make his way
the lad who rode
on the road that day

A sword in his belt
a cock–feather hat
he hailed a merchant
old and fat
'I've come to the city
to make my way'
said the lad who rode
on the road that day

'Tell me neighbor
the way to the lord
I've a mind to fight for him
stemming the horde'
the merchant shook his head
and pointed up the hill

then went back to his butcher shop
to fatten his kill

The lad rode the hill road
to the citadel
feeling slightly afraid
feeling slightly unwell
he was stopped by a guard
and told him his plan
to leave the lad behind
in search of the man

He studied the sword
sharp, shiny and pearled
and the fleet feathered shaft
the sharp point of his world
he donned a coat of cold steel
and learned the warrior's way
the lad who rode the hill road
that day

Soon he marched off to serve
in the war of his lord
to quell the rebellion
turn back the horde
he bloodied his blade
on a lad with a mace

his shield turned the blow
his sword the sad face

The horror, the battle
the blood on the dirt
the lad hugging his chest
hiding his hurt
then death brushed his fair hair
'I'll show you the way'
said he to the boy
that had killed that day

But the lad raised his sword
'get thee gone from me!
I will live to be one hundred
and fifty-three
and if ever I see
your sickle appear
I'll slice it in half
and cause thee to fear'

The dark figure smiled and bowed
but death is never cow-towed
'I tell you my friend
you'll beg me often and loudly
before the end
'For you'll not always be
the young lad I see

'You'll wish I were with you
to show you the way
oh boy who became a man this day'
And after that hour
he fought hard and he rose
a captain of men
sharp weapons, fine clothes
he crippled and killed
as if to rival his foe
seeing the lad with the mace
the face after his blow

His orders grew sterner
the attack of a town
its people to slay
its buildings burn down
he severed and slew
till the townsfolk were clay
the soldier who murdered
his meaning that day

For arms then soured
as he saw the stark fact
that his pogrom on these people
was a coward's act
stemming from the raging
of his own inner storm

now quiet and distant
confused and forlorn

So he rode back from battle
with the spoils of war
the people rushed to their windows
they ran to their doors
they hailed him, 'Renfrew!
proud and true!'
and one hundred maidens
were his to woo

But their was no maid for him
this man battle–born
was trapped by the truths
that death had forewarned

They hailed him, 'Renfrew!'
and sang his praise
in the morning's mist
in those days of days

Well, time sped on
seeking its end
and our hero grew older
he couldn't pretend
he had the strength left
to contend with his fate

his life had been death
his love had been hate

He sits in the corner
of a tavern with a cat
his hair has turned gray
his stomach turned fat
he stutters as he tells
of the days of his fame
but no one remembers
the warrior's name

No one longer remembers
the city he slew
they laugh at the tales
of the dotard, Renfrew
he begs and he pleads
for death to show him the way
and dreams of the lad
who rode the road that day

The Wooden Box

A wooden box with dust and web
sits in a corner bare
in room where once a burning wick
through rays to ease the care
in chamber once where joy was found
as side by side they lay
and hugged sweet secrets
from that sturdy box
and blessed a child's day

'Come with me! Come with me!'
she'd say again and again
'and together we'll discover
the world of men
where wars are fought
and debts are sought
and feelings and fancies
are dearly hard bought'

'No, no' said the lad
'I do not wish to know'
though deep in his heart
he wished he could go
but the box held him tight

for within it was set

all the dreams they shared

the memories they kept

The box held their troth –

the vows they did take

and also the promises

they pledged not to break

the room held the strength

of a fair mother's arm

close holding her children

to calm their alarm

'Come with me! Come with me!'

she pleaded some more

'and together we'll discover

what lies out that door

what ways we can go

what deeds we can know

what sinful injustices

we can lay low!'

Twice in vain he denied her

but the sadder she got

the faster his wooden resolve

was to rot

quick scanning the box
that still held their spell
'then tomorrow,' he sighed
'tomorrow farewell'

On the day they departed
in the box they did leave
their dreams and their secrets
to protect them from thieves
with their loves and their fears
they shut the lid tight
and opening the portal
they blew out the light

What fared on that journey
there are none here that know
though at the end of their path –
a repast of woe
for to the cottage there came
a maid with child
her skin mirror white
her manner quite mild

She'd returned to the room
and there rested herself
on top of that box
containing their wealth

she trembled while stooping
but open it she must
just enough to see
that its contents was dust

She labored for hours
and the midwifes were cross
for both mother and child
in one moment were lost
'She didn't have the strength –
we should have known
to give birth to a baby
when not yet full grown'

She didn't have the strength
aye that was plain
she had looked in that box
and had seen there her pain
He returned to the cottage
he had lost her somewhere
and their baby she carried
the sweet lady he would marry
by the box he must find her
he hoped it to be
in the room she would greet him
gaily and happily

By the box he did find her

in a box dressed in white

but the greeting she gave him

was not his respite

she sleeps now in secret

deep underground

and the young man that sought her

is not to be found

He's returned to the world

alone and bereft

his dreams and his fears

in the room he has left

his loves and his hates

to protect them from theft

but the promises they played with

as they laid side by side

in a box he buried

with his child and bride

Amric Loves the Night

Amric loves the night they say
And nightly from his earthen grave
He rises forth and ventures north
To haunt the sacred river's course

Where oak and elm and rowan twine
'Round deep and darkling knotted pine
The grove they call there 'Lover's End'
There Amric walks the woods again

'Faith – Faith' in a mournful tone
The ancient wraith is heard to moan
Where sage and thyme and clover grows
Where stone–cut Estulwaning flows

'Twas long ago that Amric strolled
Amidst those trees in autumn's cold
A love, his heart to hold that night
Enfold her in the dimming light

The setting sun was bright orange–red
And shimmered on the river's bed
When swift he paced in 'Lover's End'
In a glen where Estulwane still wends

Quick brown–dry snaps brought footsteps fast
His o'er late love had come at last
He stood there to meet her to greet her and say
'You've tarried my lovely 'tis long past the day'

His Faith was fifteen, her witch–wood hair
About her shoulders bounced on air
Running to hug him she clung to him tight
And there they lay in the dim starlight

Amric remembered the days of their youth
The times they had played the hurts he had soothed
Six years her elder he held her to be
The rarest flower the fairest to see

Yes! Amric loved those nights when long
Long he'd hold her till the dawn
Alone, their love or so he thought
But that eve's bliss was dearly bought

For through the trees on that dark night
The autumn east–wind howled with fright
Young Faith was betrayed a smithy's rage
Had wrought for her a jealous cage

Den the blacksmith's 'prentice boy
Had followed her unto their joy

And there he spied his heart's desire
And planned for Faith her funeral pyre

Many's the time within their town
Den watched her walk and followed 'round
The shops in hopes the lust to tell
That close within his coal–heart dwelled

Face of soot and hands of steel
Her soft skin he longed to feel
The unmarred whiteness of her arms
That sun–like likeness of her charms

But her tryst there it scored Den's heart
Behind a bush he squat apart
Chewing the bone the gristle of spite
Vowing with his blade to strike!

Amric stroked Faith's tangled hair
And laughter woke without despair
Within that cold he felt no chill
Within her arms he felt no ill

'Soon' she said 'We shall be wed
When your father's fears are fully fled'
Then raising a blanket up over her head
They rested on their forest bed

The blanket shroud it deadened the sound
Of the approaching closing heinous hound
The blade of desire leapt from its sheath
And red-kissed the sleeping child at peace

Not one sigh or muffled cry
Was heard as Amric's Faith died
But he awakened as from a dream
And in torment grasped the deadly scene

In their struggle the blade fell free
And Amric over his knee bent he
Who slew his Faith to the river's bed
He crushed the creature to its death

Swift within that bobbing wave
Den had found his jagged grave
Down the stream his corse did dance
To please death's wholly wholesome glance

Still beside his black-eyed flower
Amric knelt one final hour
He felt the coldness of his loss
He felt the coming of the frost

With that knife that pruned her life
He sought an answer to his strife

With bright steel-sharp he sliced his arms
And dealt himself sore mortal harms

Soft he laid beside her there
Soft wept into her witch-wood hair
Mingled and joined their blood blood red
Forming their eternal bed...

And now of autumn nights it's told
That man and beast both once thought bold
Are afraid to face in that leafless place
The wraith still searching for his Faith

Yes! Amric loves the night they say
And nightly from his earthen grave
He rises forth and ventures north
To haunt the sacred river's course

A Drinking Song

A young maid's breast this soft tipped crest
no hill 'tis fairer to win
though there are some who prefer a plum
to the shame of all their kin

High ditty Ho to conquest we go
in tavern amidst the chattel
where wenches are fine as fine as red wine
so a fool was heard to prattle

A man's no qualms to take up arms
and cut and slice and hack
but better is beer when thirst is near
and wheat cakes in a stack

High ditty Ho a drinking we go
and ventures in the street
to flog the dog and skin the hog
and eat its juicy meat

When one is young he has no tongue
to speak of tales gory
when one grows old though not as bold
the stories he tells are glory

High ditty Ho a sleeping we go
our heads all filled with ale
to dream sweet dreams and magic scenes
that cause our world to pale!